Overworked and Overwhelmed Employees

Consequences of Excessive Work in Business

Author: Dr. Iris Marie Mack, PhD, EMBA

Co-author: Wonjae Lee

Have you ever wondered if what you feel after a 65-hour work week is valid? Do other people feel all the stress, anxiety, and irritation too? Are you tired of feeling this way and want to change things up? Well, if so, this book is for you!

In our book, we discuss how working excessively can make you feel and how to shake that bad energy off. Working hard is always good. It keeps you busy, exercises your brain, and keeps you on your toes. But, of course, it should be done in moderation, and our book will teach you exactly that!

What you will learn in this book:

- What exactly is excessive workload
- The causes of excessive workload
- The causes of stress in the workplace
- Psychological and physical symptoms of work-related stress
- IIow work-related stress can overwhelm you and impact your life
- Methods to overcome work-related stress
- Some real-life stories of overwhelmed and overworked employees
- Job satisfaction level of overwhelmed and overworked employees
- And much more!

CONTENTS

INTRODUCTION

Are you the type of person who worries too much? Do you often feel overwhelmed and overworked on the job? Is your boss tough on you? Do you seem to have a never-ending stream of work to complete before the day ends?

This book is perfect for you. Learn how to effectively manage the stress that excessive workload can cause, understand why it happens in the first place, and know what the effects of the stress are.

Workload stress is often caused by working excessively long hours in or out of the office. There are several reasons for this, including taking on extra work to pay off bills or gain a promotion. Whatever causes the stress, it may prove to be damaging to our health and productivity. (Eblin, 2014)

Stress in the workplace can be detrimental to our productivity on the job. It can make us feel demotivated, insignificant, and helpless. But it doesn't end there; we carry this stress home and let it affect our relationships outside of the workplace too. It makes us feel agitated, tired, and completely worn out. Consequently, we end up isolating ourselves and damage close relationships.

hoto credit: Unsplash

Stress can affect our physical health as well and may cause heart attacks, weight gain, chest pain, and muscular tension, among other things. All of this, of course, builds up and makes us less able to perform our jobs effectively, as well as takes a toll on other aspects of life. (Sehnert, 1981)

Oftentimes, people turn to drugs or alcohol to ease the tension and stress of a long day at work, and the harmful effects of this on our lives are also explored in this book. Whether you work for a company that overworks and under compensates you or you're a manager trying to figure out the psyche of your employees, this book is for you.

CHAPTER 1: DEFINITION OF HEAVY/EXCESSIVE WORKLOAD

> Excessive workload is when the company an employee works for burdens them with too much work and often too little time to complete the work. (Best10ResumeWriters, 2019)

1.1 WHY DOES THIS HAPPEN?

There are many reasons why employees may be burdened with excessive workload. Let's explore some of them:

- The company they work for wants to stay small but needs a lot of work done. So, instead of outsourcing or hiring more employees, they may just assign the extra work to the employees who already work for them, even if it's not part of their job description.
- The industry the company operates in may be a niche or located in a particular area where it's difficult to find prospective employees with the right skills to fit in perfectly. Thus, the company may burden its existing employees with the extra work needed to be done.
- The industry the employee works in is highly competitive. The company will have to stay on top of their game at all times to make sure they always have the upper hand. This is very common in the game design and management consulting industries where working overtime is the norm. (Safarova, 2020)
- It is also quite common in the investment-banking sector because banks usually cater to huge corporate and wealthy clients, and everything has to be 100% perfect. These bankers usually end up working over 100 hours a week, which is a lot, compared to the standard 40-hour week. (Brodie, 2019)

1.2 WHY EMPLOYEES PUT UP WITH THIS

- Employees may be inclined to work excessively because they feel insecure about their job. They may feel that if they don't do the extra work, the company will simply replace them with someone who will.
- The company may be offering incentives to the employee to do the extra work. Even though the employee knows it will be extremely difficult to work those many hours or do a certain task in a limited time, they may still take it on because they need the extra money or the vacation time offered later in the job. (DiFonzo, 2015)
- Employees may also want to rise up the ranks and get promoted as fast as they can, and working more than they can handle or even more than is good for their health may very well be the only way to do this. (Cooper, 2020)
- Working long hours is often associated with being loyal to the company you work for. The boss may see it as commitment, and this helps the employee get promoted, get better perks, or a higher salary.
- Employees may often feel that they cannot say no to their boss. If they do, they may be excluded from the most interesting or esteemed projects, and their boss may not respect them. They may also be pressured by the boss or other employees, and, thus, cannot reject the extra work. (Weisinger & Pawliw-Fry, 2015)

Of course, it's never just one of these reasons why an employee is overworked. It's usually a combination of a few of these. Oftentimes, the employee will take on the excessive load of work without complaining, but this eventually leads to mental and physical health issues. These issues are not just detrimental for the workers but affect their family, friends, colleagues, and even the company itself. (Argenal, 2020)

The managers of a company must be ready to listen to the complaints of their employees without bias or judgment. They should create an environment where the employees are free to draw the line on where the workload crosses a reasonable amount. (Peters, 2014)

1.3 QUANTITY OVER QUALITY

If an employee is given too much to do, they may start prioritizing completing the work, instead of really focusing on each task. This may lead to mistakes that could cost the company a lot of money or their respect and brand name in the market. If the employee is focused on just finishing the work, it may get done eventually, but not with the level of care that should have been given. (Hawkins, 2020)

For example, if a baker normally bakes three cakes per day, but is now being pressured to bake eight per day, they may get it done, but perhaps the icing on top will not be as detailed, or the flavor may be a little off. These little things may translate into a loss of earnings for the bakery, as customers may start noticing these things and prefer to shop elsewhere.

1.4 WORK -LIFE BALANCE

A work-life balance is essential in situations such as these. A good work-life balance would be one where employees are given the flexibility to choose an appropriate amount of time allotted to work and to leisure. This can help the employees feel as if they have some control over their work and their lives, and can actually further motivate them to do their job better. (Harvard Business Review, 2019)

Photo credit: Unsplash

CHAPTER 2: HOW A HEAVY WORKLOAD CAUSES STRESS

When employees are overworked, their motivation to complete those tasks actually decreases. This is because they may feel as if they're working and *working and working – to no end!* The employee may feel as if they aren't getting much done, even if they are. This is because after completing one task, they'll then look at the ten other tasks yet to be completed and feel as if nothing has been accomplished. (Roger & Petrie, 2016)

2.1 CAUSES OF STRESS IN THE WORKPLACE

2.1.1 Too much work

Sometimes employees may be given more work than they can handle. Just thinking of all the extra work piling up as they continue to work can cause high blood pressure and a lot of stress. Employees may not be offered any help or moral support, and this will lead to a feeling of loneliness and helplessness. They may not have any colleagues around them who can help them out and, thus, feel overworked and overwhelmed. (Eblin, 2014)

2.1.2 No training

An employee may be given work that's not in their job description for reasons stated in the previous chapter. They may not possess the skills required to complete the task successfully and, thus, will have to spend long hours first learning how to do it and then actually completing the task. Lack of training can cause a loss for the company and every single worker in that company. Overworking has to become an outright choice in order to catch up the work required of them.

This may make them feel isolated and confused, especially if the company itself doesn't offer any special training, and the employee has to figure out the work all on their own. (Smith, 2018)

2.1.3 Monotonous work

An employee may just sit day after day at their desk while new work is constantly assigned to them. This may make them feel as if they have no control over their work or life and demotivate them to complete any task. (Csikszentmihalyi, 2000)

2.1.4 Job insecurity

The company may be making cuts, and out of fear of being laid off, the employee may agree to do extra work that they cannot handle. In addition to the stress of keeping their job, they will now be stressed to finish tasks at the given deadlines. Their boss often pressures employees and the employees can't refuse to avoid losing their jobs or getting bad performance reviews. (Segal, 2020)

2.1.5 Unappreciated employees

If an employee isn't appreciated after completion of a set number of tasks, they may be very demotivated to work further. They may feel as if they're not an integral part of the company and maybe easily replaced. Being demotivated, they'll work less, and as the work piles up, so does the stress. (Bush & Peters, 2020)

2.1.6 Necessity

An employee may agree to the work because they need the extra money, or are in fear of losing their job. However, the reality may be that they cannot cope with all the extra work. They may constantly think about how to not lose the job and how to earn extra money, and, thus, add stress to their life.

2.1.7 Unrealistic deadlines

Unrealistic deadlines may also be a factor causing stress related to the workplace. If an employee is assigned a task, they'll have to work day and night to complete it on time; they may feel rushed and overwhelmed (Dennis, 2007). The example of unrealistic deadlines is well displayed in the game industry. They have a term, "crunch time," which means that the video game managers bottleneck tasks, making the employees rush to finish the tasks for the development that are nearly impossible to finish on time.

2.1.8 Priority confusion

If multiple managers give multiple tasks to the same employee to complete in a short time, the employee won't know which one to prioritize, especially if each manager insists it should be their task. This will cause stress to build up, as they may not be able to complete all tasks at the same time.

It's hard to expect outstanding productivity if you're working too much. A Stanford research paper found that people who worked 70 hours per week didn't actually get more work done than their peers who worked 56 hours per week. Excessive work will only cause a loss for the employee and the company itself. This is because the employee will be too stressed to give 100% to every project. They may then start prioritizing quantity over quality of work done, which, in turn, translates to a loss for the company. (Basil, 2019)

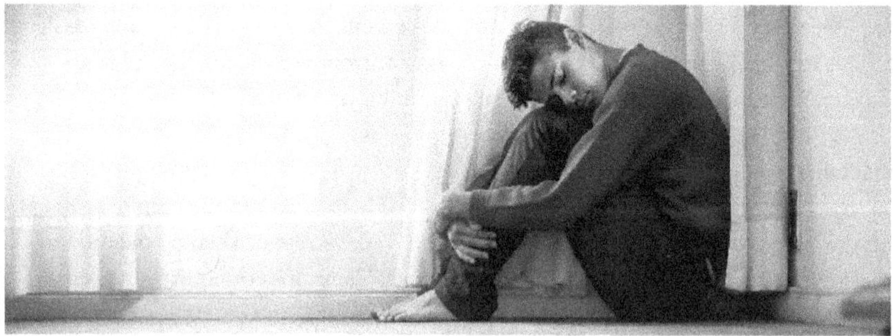

Photo credit: Pixabay

A stressed employee will be unmotivated to work and won't be able to give their full effort and dedication. They'll be spread out too thin, instead of really focusing on one project at a time.

This means they may make more mistakes. This can be a major loss for the company, as they can lose clients, profits, and their standing in the market. (Bush & Peters, 2020)

2.1.9 Unmotivated

If the employee is not being paid extra for the excessive workload they're expected to deliver, they'll have no reason to be motivated to complete it on time or do it diligently. (Thomas, 2009)

2.2 SYMPTOMS OF WORK-RELATED STRESS

If any employee is stressed about their work, they may not be able to sleep properly. Staying up all night and then reporting back to work in the morning means their productivity levels will drastically decrease. They won't be able to complete the tasks given to them, and, thus, the stress will increase.

The stress may result in trouble concentrating on tasks, as the employee may be distracted by all the other tasks that have to be completed or just a feeling of doom and helplessness.

Even outside of the workplace, the stress may haunt them. They may feel irritable, annoyed, and not be able to enjoy themselves in their leisure time. The employee may just keep thinking about all the work that has yet to be completed, putting a strain on their life outside of work. (Segal, 2020)

Photo credit: Pixabay

CHAPTER 3: EFFECTS OF EXCESSIVE WORKLOAD ON YOUR PHYSICAL HEALTH AND SOCIAL LIFE

Stress is defined as the body's coping mechanism when it senses danger. When working properly, stress can be good for you. It may give you that extra energy to complete your homework due in the morning, or save your life by driving you to run away from a wild bear wandering in your backyard. However, if your stress levels increase too much, it may become a problem. (Segal, 2020; Wilkinson & Pickett, 2020)

Excessive work-related stress can be extremely detrimental to your health, especially in the long run but also in the short run. It decreases motivation to work, productivity in and out of the workplace, and a general sense of being excited to live. It can cause relationships to fall apart and put a strain on family life. (Felton, 2020)

3.1 PSYCHOLOGICAL SYMPTOMS OF WORK-RELATED STRESS

If an employee is faced with too much work-related stress, they may face

- Depression
- Anxiety
- Irritability
- Pessimism
- Feeling like a failure or not good enough
- Problems with concentration or focusing on one task
- Feeling unmotivated, overwhelmed, and constantly rushed…

These people may make rushed, bad, or uninformed decisions in and out of the workplace, which can result in personal losses or losses for the company. Stress may keep the overworked employee up at night, so their productivity the next day decreases. If they have to give a presentation in the morning, they may not be entirely ready for it, or may not be as energetic as they should be. (Chiesa, 2019)

3.2 PHYSICAL SYMPTOMS OF WORK-RELATED STRESS

Work-related stress might induce fatigue in the employee, along with headaches, muscular tension, chest pain, rapid heart rate, and lower immunity, leading to frequent flu or colds, constipation, weight problems, and reproductive issues, among others. (Segal, 2020)

The stressed and overworked employee will be too unmotivated to work or too tired from overthinking and not sleeping enough, and this will cause problems for the individual in the workplace. They'll be far less productive than their colleagues, which may cause embarrassment or bullying to occur. The employee's boss may not be happy and may start disliking the employee, risking any chances of promotion.

Employees who are too stressed will most likely have issues outside of the workplace as well.

- ☐ The stress may cause a strain on family life. The individual may be too tired after spending all day at work to play with their children or spend time with their partner or other family members, causing further problems.
- ☐ They may be too tired or unmotivated to go out with friends, attend weddings, parties, and other functions. This will cause isolation, which is also one cause of stress.

Photo credit: Pexels

3.3 EXERCISE AND STRESS

People who are too stressed may be tense throughout the day and feel tired and unmotivated. This will result in a loss of motivation to go on a jog or to the gym. If one sits at a desk all day, working on a laptop, their physical activity will most likely be minimal.

Exercise is essential to beat a multitude of health problems, such as strokes, high blood pressure, and arthritis, among others. It helps pump endorphins, which are the brain's feel-good neurotransmitters, is a good way to meditate and improves your mood, along with reducing stress. If one is too stressed, they miss out on all the health benefits exercise has to offer. (Nanavati, 2016)

3.4 SUBSTANCE ABUSE

People usually turn to drugs or drinking when under immense stress, and this will be detrimental to the employee's health and relationships. It may deter the employee from sleeping and staying asleep, waking up for the office and meetings on time, being 100% productive at all times, being prepared for presentations, completing all work at the required time, and keeping healthy office relationships. (Harrison, 2020)

3.5 THE STRAIN ON SOCIAL LIFE

The use of drugs or excessive drinking may also cause tension between the employee and their family or friends. It can cause the employee to neglect their children. This is possible in many ways, such as not

- ☐ helping out on homework assignments,
- ☐ feeding the child at the proper time,
- ☐ making sure the child has clean clothes, or
- ☐ putting the child to bed at a suitable bedtime. (McCoy & Keen, 2013)

The employee taking drugs or drinking may also harm the relationship between them and their spouse/partner. They may become angry or agitated quickly and even physically abusive at times. (Haraway & Hansen, 2004)

One tends to self-isolate when dependent on drugs or alcohol, so the individual may avoid friends and family. They may not show up at events, gatherings, or funerals, and may become dependent on the substance they're abusing. This will cause a multitude of problems for the individual at home and at work and, consequently, they may even have to go to rehab.

3.6 LONGER HOURS BUT LESSER PRODUCTIVITY

If an individual is overworked, they may actually be facing decreased productivity. This may be because the brain is tired and needs a rest. John Pencavel from Stanford University researched productivity linked to long hours and found that productivity per hour actually decreases after the 50 hours per week mark. He also found that after 55 hours a week, productivity decreases so sharply that there really isn't any benefit to putting in more hours. (Pencavel, 2018)

South Korea is the country that recently started limiting the *work hours to 52 hours per week since 2018.* Before the regulation, South Korean companies often forced employees to do overtime after their regular working hours and do activity with their boss during the weekend that's not related to the task in their workplace.

Excessive workload on an individual may also cause them to
- sleep more
- eat too much or too little
- procrastinate
- be negligent in and outside of work
- be irresponsible
- engage in many other unhealthy habits

Photo credit: Pixabay

CHAPTER 4: THE KEY TO MANAGING HEAVY WORKLOAD – TIPS AND MEASURES

To lead a healthy life, one must find the right balance between work and leisure. Work keeps our minds busy and well, and gives us independence and control over our lives. It challenges us to better ourselves, to learn new skills, and meet people from different backgrounds. *However, how much work is too much work? And can it be harmful?*

From reading the previous chapters, we can conclude that, yes, absolutely, too much work can be harmful. It can cause psychological and physical disorders, such as **anxiety and stress**, and lower immunity and weakened eyesight, respectively.

Thus, it's imperative that we learn how to manage the heavy workload we get, and the stress that comes along with it. (Harvard Business Review, 2019)

4.1 MANAGING THE HEAVY WORKLOAD

Practice the following points to manage your heavy load of work and the stress that comes along with it. These techniques will help you keep your stress levels to a minimum.

4.1.1 Know your limits

Recognize your limitations and know where to stop. Identify when your work is consuming your life, and you barely have any time or energy for other activities. Make sure you stop there. It's good to push your limits occasionally, but doing so constantly can leave you feeling drained and unmotivated. (Odimba, 2020)

4.1.2 Learn to say no.

If your boss is overburdening you with work, you won't be able to do any of it with full concentration. If it's too much for you, let your boss know. Tell them that it's beyond what you can accomplish in a day. There's no shame there; we're humans, not robots! (Zahariades, 2017)

Photo credit: Pexels

4.1.3 Don't procrastinate

Start with your work as soon as you get it. This will build a good work ethic and make sure all your work isn't left for the last minute. This is also a good precaution because if something goes wrong and you just have the last few minutes before the deadline to finish it, you'll have a head start. **If you start early, you finish early.** (Burka & Yuen, 2008)

4.1.4 Set a routine

Having a set routine allows you to stay in control of your day. It makes it easy for us to map out all the tasks we have to complete. It can also be comforting to know that no matter what we do throughout the day, lunch is at a specific time and so is dinner. This would also be comforting if, after sitting behind a desk for 11 hours a day, you know that when you get home, you have to take your dog for a walk, which also gives you a chance to unwind all the built-up stress and tension. (Clear, 2018)

4.1.5 To-do lists

To-do lists can really help us declutter our minds and get over feeling overwhelmed. It helps us stay in touch with everything done and everything yet to do. This can also help keep track of the progress you make throughout the day. The feeling of satisfaction you get when you cross off an item on your to-do list is a good stress reliever. (Zahariades, 2016)

4.1.6 Follow that routine

We, as humans, aren't perfect. We make mistakes, we mess up, and, most of all, we slack off. It's very easy to fall off the right track, but that's where the test of your willpower comes in. You must try to establish a routine and follow it. This doesn't mean being unnecessarily harsh on yourself. If one day you don't perform as well, skip your morning jog or eat unhealthily, just don't beat yourself up too much about it. Start fresh and determined the next day. (Clear, 2018)

4.1.7 Be flexible

Following a routine has so many great benefits, but sometimes we may feel as if we're stuck in a rut. If this happens, try changing up what you do every day. Perhaps jog in the evening some days instead of the morning, or drink a smoothie instead of oatmeal every day. Routines are good to keep around, but if yours becomes stressful, be flexible and don't be afraid to switch it up. (Miller, 2020)

4.1.8 Share your worries

Sometimes, the best thing for you to do is share your worries with someone you trust, whether it's your partner, friend, or family member. Talking about your feelings helps you feel lighter and relieves some of the excess burden and stress. (Carbonell & Winston, 2016)

4.1.9 Get some exercise

Exercise helps the body destress. It increases your overall health and pumps the brain full of endorphins, the feel-good neurotransmitters. It can help improve your mood and is just as calming as meditation. With a busy schedule, it can be difficult to fit in regular exercise, so try doing it three or four times a week. (Nanavati, 2016)

4.1.10 Healthy diet

A healthy diet is very important to decrease stress that comes from work or otherwise. You might even get a chance to unwind after a long day at work by cooking your favorite recipe. Many junk foods or the food we get from fast-food chains can cause our blood pressure and heart rate to increase significantly, as they contain high amounts of fat, salt, and calories. Foods such as eggs, dark chocolate, and turmeric have been scientifically proven to reduce stress and, thus, help us relax after a tiring day. (Crichton-Stuart, 2018)

4.1.11 Get creative

When you've been working constantly for hours on end, sometimes, a change is good. Do something you enjoy:

- ☐ write a poem
- ☐ read a book
- ☐ draw a picture
- ☐ dance
- ☐ listen to some music
- ☐ volunteer
- ☐ paint your kitchen wall
- ☐ bake a cake for a friend, family member, colleague – or even for a homeless person!

Get your creative juices flowing and make sure you get your mind off of work for a while. If you keep thinking about all the things you have yet to do while you're painting, drawing, or baking, you'll end up tiring your brain more and stressing yourself during your relaxation time.

4.1.12 Visit a doctor

If you feel as if the workload has become too much for you to handle and no method of calming your nerves is working, it may be helpful to visit a health care professional. Your doctor may be able to help you with some techniques to calm yourself down so you don't take on as much stress. They may treat this by giving you medication, nutritional supplements, herbal remedies, or simply teaching you some easy exercises or meditation techniques, such as slow breathing and counting to 10. (Askin, 2014)

4.1.13 Working from home

If you're a freelancer or someone who works remotely (i.e., from home), and you find yourself easily stressed by the overburdening amounts of work you have to do every day, you may find these simple hacks very useful. (Detjens, 2020)

In the case of people who have an office job, COVID-19 pandemic has proven that working from home doesn't decrease workers' productivity and respect workers' work-life balance. Working from home shows the possibility of how the company's working condition could change soon.

4.1.14 Wake up early

When you wake up early in the morning, the distractions are minimal. Your friends and family may be asleep, so there's less chance of being interrupted. It's a good idea to wake up earlier than everyone else if you share a living space.

This will give you some quiet time to think, work, exercise, or just get things in order. Of course, when you wake up early, you can also start working early. If you have a heavy workload, **the earlier you start, the earlier you can finish.** (Traub, 2013)

4.1.15 Plan

Start with planning your day. This could be a mental note of all the tasks you have to do in the day or a to-do list. Either way, planning helps you clear up your mind and relax. You can then be sure you haven't missed anything and do all your work systematically. (Burchard, 2018)

Photo credit: Pexels

4.1.16 Start with the hardest task

This will help put that task you've been dreading out of the way, so you don't waste any more energy stressing about it. After this, you'll be free to do other smaller or easier tasks, and this will help you not feel overwhelmed every time you think of all you have left to do.

Especially if you finish a harder task first when you're in good condition, you'll feel a greater sense of accomplishment and give yourself inspiration and energy to go further toward the next task. The statement made in this section is based on recent studies. (Iliaca, 2019)

This topic can cause controversy because, regardless of the result of the research, people will have a different preference for handling their tasks.

4.1.17 Leave your house

It's difficult to unglue yourself from your computer screen when you have excess amounts of work every day, but this is extremely important. Go for a run, go shopping, or visit a friend. Fresh air is always good for you. This can help you unwind and refocus on your work, making sure you can give 100% to every task you complete. (Cohen, 2011)

One of the advantages of working from home is that you can spend more time for yourself. Sticking yourself in front of the computer screen will give you a similar experience from working in the office. Refresh yourself by going for a walk or a drive that gives you happiness.

4.2 FOR MANAGERS

Chief Executive Officers (CEOs) have a responsibility for improving the working environment for their employees. This is directly connected to the workers' sense of duty toward their company and their productivity. In fact, they actually have a legal obligation to make sure the work they give their employees isn't harmful to their health. (Peters, 2014)

Managers must make sure their employees aren't overworked, and this would benefit the company's revenue and reputation by making the employees more careful and productive. If you're a manager and have realized your employees may be facing excessive workload, make sure you do the following:

4.2.1 Work-life balance

This is where employees are allowed to maintain a good balance between the time and effort given to work and that given to life outside of work, such as family and friends. These breaks

- ☐ help the employees to unwind and relax, and
- ☐ ensure they come into work the next morning with a fresh mind, ready to give 100% to their work.

It also lets your employees know you care about them and want to protect them from mental and physical health issues. This will motivate employees further, and they'll start enjoying their work. This will increase productivity. (Harvard Business Review, 2019)

4.2.2 Give your employees time off

Offer paid time off to an employee for a major life event, such as undergoing surgery or having a child. Let your employees pick their own timings if possible, and make sure your employees are taking their vacation days off. A few days off won't hurt the productivity of the business as much as a demotivated employee will (Lopez, 2017). Every company in the world has a duty of providing mandatory vacation for their employees. Mandatory vacation days consist of many pros over the cons. Thinking of the *importance of work-life balance* will give you a better understanding of this policy.

4.2.3 Training

Training your employees saves them the hassle of learning new skills all by themselves when you give them a task they've never done before. This will let them complete the task in less

time and make it much easier for them to get their job done. A motivated and trained employee who isn't stressed will be far more productive. (Employee Benefits, 2017)
It's important to give yourself a break, even if you have a lot of work. Get up, walk around, go outside, and breathe in some fresh air. *Make sure you keep yourself hydrated and stay positive!*

Photo credit: Pexels

CHAPTER 5: DO CULTURES REALLY PLAY A ROLE IN ADJUSTING WORKING HOURS?

Culture encompasses the intellectual, spiritual, and moral beliefs of a country or specific place. Cultures play an important role in adjusting work hours and overtime work. Every country has different laws and norms—these laws and norms mold office culture. (Meyer, 2014)

A country's ethics and moral code shape
- a business's managerial style
- human resource management practices
- communication in and outside of work
- motivation
- people's work ethics
- labor laws

Some countries have laws putting a cap on the maximum number of hours an employee can work per week, and if work-related emails and calls are allowed after work hours have ended. Cultural values and laws in a country matter immensely in how many working hours per week an employee is allowed. (Khan & Law, 2018)

5.1 OECD COMPARISON

The chart below, taken from the Organization for Economic Cooperation and Development (OECD), shows that people in Northern European countries such as Norway, Denmark, and the Netherlands work relatively less than in other countries. Working hours can be a good indicator of the welfare in the country and the core industry that the country has. (OECD, 2018)

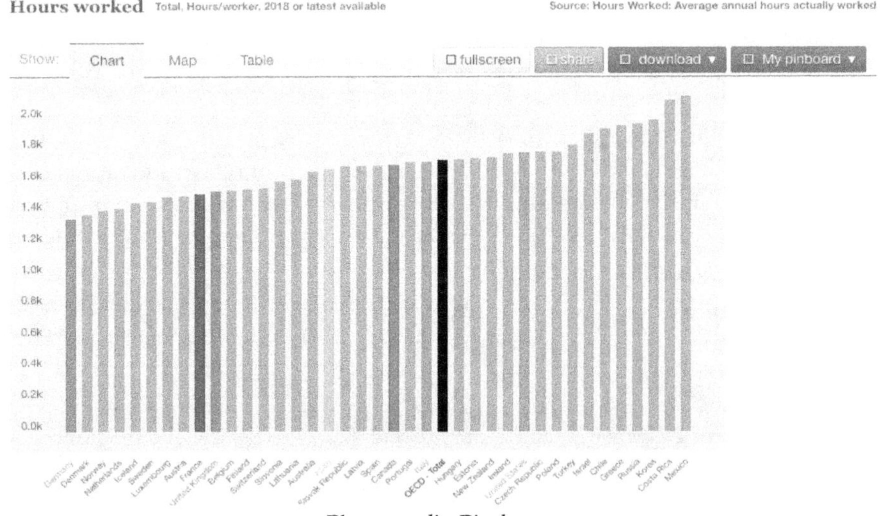

Photo credit: Pixabay

Northern European countries are well known for their generous welfare systems, and the service industry is one of the core industries in the country. Thus, the cost of labor is more expensive than in other countries.

For developing countries, the ratio of the manufacturing industry is higher than in developed countries. In addition, GDP is lower in developing countries than in developed countries. Hence, the cost of labor is cheaper in developing countries. As each of the factors is integrated, it makes a good condition for the excessive number of working hours.

Statutory holidays also vary according to the country. For example, the mean annual working hours per employee is
- 2,255 in Mexico
- 1,993 in South Korea
- 1,783 in the United States
- 1,363 in Germany

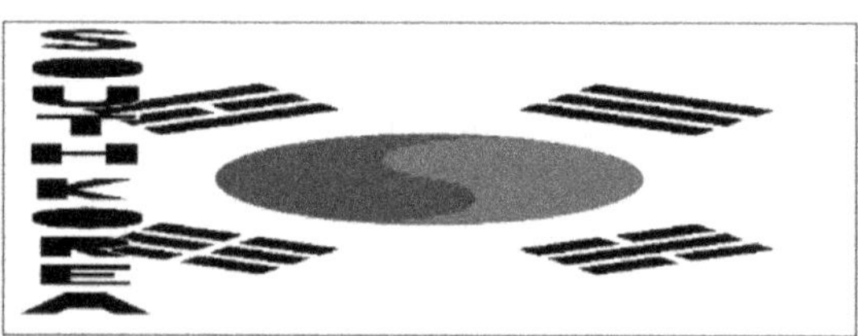

Photo credit: Pixabay

5.2 SOUTH KOREA

According to the OECD chart, South Korea is ranked at 3rd place for working 1,993 mean annual hours/worker. South Korea has developed a sort of "workaholic culture" due to rapid industrialization after the 1950 Korean War. In South Korea, workers cannot leave the office until their boss leaves the office. Workers are often called by the boss on the weekend to do extra work or to do outdoor activity together. (Brindle, 2020; Gonzalez & Lee, 2019)

Employees are almost forced to follow the boss's suggestion, and allowance is not commonly given for that, unlike in the United States. An employment contract is made when the employee is recruited to the company. However, many offices in South Korea often violate the terms and conditions in the contract by forcing the workers to come to the office on the workers' off days. Just like this situation, the exploitation of labor happens frequently, and they don't get any adequate reward for finishing extra tasks. South Korean employees also suffer with the email or call out of work hours and they are never paid for responding to those calls and emails.

As the Ministry of Employment and Labor in South Korea recognized the seriousness of the overwork and its consequences, they decided to limit employees' work to 52 hours per week. Lawmakers expect that this policy will improve the firms' productivity, increase the number of jobs, and potentially the country's birth rate.

5.2.1 Change in working hours

All this overtime work and undercompensation has taken a toll on employees in South Korea, as the country now has the highest rates of suicide in the world. However, pledges have been made for change in the average hours an employee can be called to work for. (Necek & Hoorpah, 2016)

A new law passed states that *South Koreans can work a maximum of 52 hours a week*, a decrease from the previous 68 hours a week law. There have been mixed emotions about this, as some people are happy, but others fear they will be called in anyway, and legally, they cannot be compensated for this. (Smith, 2018; Strait Times, 2018)

Before the 52-hour week law was passed in South Korea, Koreans were working about
- 300 more hours a year than employees in Italy or in the United States
- 700 more hours a year than employees in Germany and in Norway

However, even though Koreans were working far more hours than many others, this did not guarantee extra productivity. In 2014, Korea's labor productivity was US$31.90 per hour, compared to the OECD's average of US$49.

5.3 GERMANY

Germany and its laws can then contrast all of this. Germans generally believe in quality over quantity. They believe in working fewer hours and producing more. **When Germans work, they focus 100%** on the work they're doing. (Hampshire, 2017)

In German business culture, when an employee is working, that's all they should be doing. They shouldn't be distracted by social media or colleagues. Such behavior is obviously frowned upon in other countries such as the United States, but in Germany, it's absolutely unacceptable. This is why the average work hours annually in Germany are much lower compared to other countries. The completely focused work means the average German employee gets more done in less time. (Sarva, 2017)

5.3.1 Work hard and play hard

Germans believe in having lives outside of work. Once outside of the office, Germans don't work. There is very little overtime and working from home after a long day at the office. In fact, the employment ministry in Germany has banned work emails or calls out of work hours, except for emergencies.

If an employee responds to a work email or call after work hours have ended, they must be paid for the time they spend doing this. The German government has imposed this ban to protect employees from being overworked and prevent work-related stress and fatigue. (Telegraph UK, 2020)

5.4 JAPAN

On the other hand, Japan has a culture of extremely long work hours, with little to no compensation. Japanese work ethic differs greatly from that of America. Americans tend to be more laid back, but for the Japanese, it's mostly all work and no play. Japanese families tend to expect the best of the best from their family members. The pressure to work excessively to earn money and respect is higher than in most other countries. (Saiidi, 2018)

5.4.1 Overtime

Overtime is almost accepted as a norm in Japanese and Korean culture. Almost all Japanese employees work around *80 hours of overtime per month* and are hardly ever compensated for these overtime hours. Unpaid overtime is very common in Japan. To be respected at work, the culture and mindsets of people require you to work absurdly long hours. Just like South Korea, it's not acceptable to leave the office before your boss does. The highly competitive nature of the Japanese people makes it almost impossible for employees to leave before their colleagues do. (Saiidi, 2018)

5.4.2 Japanese customs

Working exceptionally long hours is embedded so deeply into Japanese culture that convenience stores actually sell clean shirts for employees who haven't had a chance to go home and change.

Furthermore, the Kodoku genre of literature in Japan focuses on the isolation of Japanese employees who don't have time to go home and meet family and friends or have any social life at all. (Yutaka & Qusumi, 2012)

It is not just Japanese companies that are forcing their employees to work this much. The Japanese people themselves tend to take fewer vacations and holidays from work, even the ones they are entitled to.

5.4.3 Longer hours, more productivity?

Japanese people believe that working longer hours means more productivity; however, this has proven to be false. Japan actually has the longest hours of work but the lowest productivity among the **G-7 nations**. The G-7 is an international intergovernmental economic organization that consists of the following 7 nations: (Feroli, 2013; Saiidi, 2018)

- Canada
- France
- Germany
- Italy
- Japan
- United Kingdom
- United States

5.4.4 The dark side of Japanese work ethic

Japan has long been known for its high suicide rates. This is because the norm is to prioritize work above all else, which leads to individuals neglecting their own health and happiness too.

The Japanese barely have any time for their personal lives, and so many go on to marry very late, or not at all. This means the number of newborns in Japan is very low, compared to other countries, and actually hit a record low in 2018: 918,397 births in the entire year. Japan has a **very high aging population** due to this. The death rates outnumber the birth rates per day by 1000. (Kyodo, 2019)

5.4.5 Karoshi

Karoshi literally means *"death by overwork."* This term is legally recognized. In Japan, suicide is often seen as an honorable way to die. Many people think that if you cannot support your family and earn money, it's better to just commit suicide. Many people also end their lives after they retire, perhaps believing they have served their purpose. Aokigahara Forest, near Mount Fuji, is known to be a hotspot for suicides. (Devlin, 2019)

5.5 GOVERNMENT INITIATIVES

The government of Japan has recognized the overworked and overwhelmed culture in its country and has made it mandatory for all employees to take at least 5 days off in a year, and for an employee to rest at the end of one day before the next day starts. (Saiidi, 2018)

Many countries are now realizing the problems of overworking their employees and have moved toward a strict approach where an employee can only work during their working hours, whether they're the standard 9-5 or different. Countries like France have even banned work-related emails and calls to employees out of work hours. These countries are also now allowing their workers to choose flexible timings for themselves. (Telegraph, 2016; Wilson, 2019)

Photo credit: Pixabay

CHAPTER 6: SOME REAL-LIFE STORIES

6.1 SOUTH KOREA

Mr. Chae Soo-hong was a manager at a food supplier, that specialized in Jangjorim, a beef dish cooked in soy sauce, which is quite popular in South Korea. His primary duty was to make sure the production was running smoothly. (Maangchi & Shulman, 2019)

South Korea implemented a structure to make sure citizens of the country work more to help get Korea back on its feet after the Korean War in 1950. This structure soon became a culture and has been that way for decades now.

This is one reason why Chae Soo-hong was so overworked. He often performed duties that weren't in his job description, such as helping other factory employees with any problems they were having, particularly those who came from overseas. He often felt as if his duties just kept on increasing, even though the company expanded from 30 employees to 80 in the 2 years Chae had worked there from 2015 to 2017.

For Chae Soo-hong, a typical working week was 6 days. He worked from 7 am to 10 pm every single day, as his wife, Park Hyun-suk, recalls. Monday to Friday, Chae Soo-hong would travel to the company's factories and supervise the production process. On Saturday, he would go to the main office and fill out paperwork.

Coming home at 10 pm, he would still not be done with his work. In fact, he would then go on to work at home. Chae's wife Park told CNN that Chae would be so tired after work, that he would spend all his time at home sleeping. Chae barely took any time off, which was evident, as his wife couldn't find a single picture of them together at first. It took her a long time to find one picture of them, and another of him in his work clothes, while being interviewed by CNN.

One Saturday morning, before Chae left for work, he complained to his wife of feeling tired, but Park did not think much of it because Chae worked so much that he was always tired. Park now regrets not taking any action because Chae didn't come home that day. Instead, his coworkers found him dead, lying on the floor in his office. He died at around 7 pm on a Saturday in August 2017. Chae was one of the hundreds of Koreans that year to die of exhaustion due to excessive workload.

So many people in South Korea die each year from excessive work that they have a word for it, "Gwarosa." It literally translates to **death by overwork**. Park receives a monthly compensation check from the company her husband worked at, but most families aren't as fortunate.

Many companies refuse to pay workplace death compensation. As men are usually the sole breadwinners of the family in South Korea, this leaves the unfortunate families mourning the death of their loved one while scrambling to make ends meet. (Kwon & Field, 2018)

6.2 CHINA

Mr. Li Jianhua died on April 23, 2014. He was a Chinese banking regulator who worked at the Chinese Banking Regulatory Commission (CRBC). Li literally worked himself to death and was praised for it.

Mr. Jianhua was born in 1965, in Baotou, located in Inner Mongolia. He studied economics in university and earned a doctorate. He was 48 years old at the time of his death, and he had been working at the bank for the past 26 years.

Li joined the communist party in 1985 and started working for the government in the department of banking regulation. He took a job at CRBC in 2005. Here, he set standards for regulating China's economic boom.

Mr. Jianhua had good reason to be overworked and extremely tense all the time. His job required him to travel to 10 provinces in China in just 6 months and meet with all 68 of China's trust companies. It was common for Li, and other employees in his department to work till midnight every single day, and so it wasn't a surprise when his death was classified as "long-time overwork."

In the days leading up to his death, Li had an attack of Shingles. *Shingles is a rash* that appears in the body when the immune system is compromised. Stress weakens the immune system, and it's believed that all the tension buildup from work most likely caused Shingles in Li. However, he is reported to have said that he couldn't go to the doctor to get it checked out because he had too much work and no time. (Carlton, 2014)

With the rash covering his body, he still went on tour to Hunan province and worked there as if nothing was wrong. One of Li's colleagues eventually found out that the rash covered his entire torso. Li asked him to keep it a secret, as he didn't want to worry others with the news.

Mr. Jianhua never discussed anything personal at work but always kept his door open for any work-related discussions a colleague may want to have. He barely had time for his family. He was always at the office working, and when he came home, he was scrambling to get work done from his house before the sun came up. After Li's death, his wife struggled to get the news to his office and coworkers because she didn't know a single person who worked with him, despite his having worked in the same office for so many years.

Li Jianhua was reported to have been found in his room, lying on the floor, in the early morning hours of April 23rd. He had been working all night, suffered from a heart attack, and eventually succumbed to it. Li died while frantically working on completing a report for his office, due in a few hours.

China is still not a fully developed country, and the general mindset of people there is that without soul-crushing work, nothing can be achieved. It is very common in China for managers and other employees to be given tasks with short deadlines that are virtually impossible to complete without working overtime.

After the death of Mr. Li Jianhua, the management committee of the company he worked at released a statement saying that all Chinese people should aspire to be like Li, and that his death was an honorable one. They also added that they were proud of Li for putting the Party and the people of China before his own needs. (Edwards, 2014; Oster, 2014)

6.3 EUROPE

Mr. Jean-Paul Rouanet was a French employee who worked at France Telecom, now known as Orange, in Annecy-le-Vieux. He had lost his job at the Enterprise agency two months prior to his death and was subsequently forced to find work at France Telecom, in the telephone platform department.

Jean-Paul had found changing jobs extremely difficult. He couldn't cope with the constant pressure from work. He often confided in his friend, who worked with him, that he couldn't take it anymore, but the company didn't care how their employees felt and how they were doing.

Jean-Paul eventually succumbed to his distress. He drove up to the lby-Sur-Chéran Viaduct, a bridge, near Annecy. He parked his car nearby, in the emergency lane of the motorway. One hundred meters above ground, Jean-Paul positioned himself to jump. People below understood what he was trying to do and started shouting at him, trying to persuade him not to jump. After some hesitation, Jean-Paul eventually jumped down and ended his life.

Police officers searched his car and found a suicide note that he had written and left for his wife and 2 children. Jean-Paul was married and had two children, one aged 12 and the other 8. In this letter, he wrote about his office life and how unhappy he was working there because it tired him out so much. The police officers read the suicide note and concluded that Jean-Paul's suicide was entirely due to being overworked, overwhelmed, and exhausted due to an excessive workload.

Jean-Paul was one of the 35 employees of France Telecom to kill themselves between 2008 and 2009. (Le Parisien, 2009; Lim, 2017)

Photo credit: Pixabay

CHAPTER 7: IMPACT OF EXCESSIVE WORKLOAD ON JOB SATISFACTION

The amount of work an employee has to complete in a set amount of time matters greatly when it comes to job satisfaction. This works both ways; giving an employee too little work can be almost as detrimental as too much work. (Kelly, 2020)

7.1 TOO LITTLE WORK

Giving an employee too little work means they won't feel challenged and motivated. It may make the employee complacent and lazy. They may feel as if the employer doesn't trust them to get the job done or think they have the skills necessary. This will also cause job dissatisfaction.

7.2 TOO MUCH WORK

The consequences of the excessive workload are extensive and extremely harmful, as seen in the previous chapter. Employees will be overworked and not have any time for their family or friends or themselves. If an employee is expected to work from morning until night, they'll eventually dread coming into work. (Eblin, 2014)

7.3 INEQUALITIES

A company may have several employees holding the same position such as a group of associates at a law firm. It may be demotivating for an employee if they notice that they're getting much more work than their colleagues, especially if they all have more or less the same skill set. There may be an imbalance between each employee, which will further demotivate them. (Durand, 2011)

Discriminating against employees based on gender or race is a practice that needs to be avoided, as it can damage the company's reputation. The evaluation of an employee must be based only on their performance.

7.4 BURNOUT

Burnout is the result of chronic stress at the workplace that hasn't been successfully dealt with. It's characterized by exhaustion and depersonalization (negativism/cynicism) and is found predominantly in caring and social professions (e.g., social workers, teachers, nurses, doctors, and dentists). (Weber & Jaekel-Reinhard, 2000)

Photo credit: Pixabay

If employees are given too much work and too little time to complete it, such as one day, they may find it extremely hard to bear. It will create ill feelings in the employee for the job and the boss. This will prevent the employee from giving 100% for the next task.

Further, after a long and tiring day, if the employee is given the same amount of work the next day, they may not be able to complete it. This is because they will be "burnt out." (Nagoski, 2020)

7.5 HEALTH FACTORS

If the health of an employee is slowly deteriorating, the employee may realize they need to quit the job. This would be termed **"turnover intention."** This is when the employee hasn't yet quit the job but is considering quitting.

If the employee has strict deadlines and needs to work day and night to complete an assigned task, for example, they may be at high risk of having a heart attack or high blood pressure. (Kennedy, 2012)

7.6 STRESS

A heavy workload also causes a lot of stress for people. Stress can affect people mentally and physically. This means they can face physical problems such as a *stroke, muscular tension, chest pain, rapid heart rate, and lower immunity, leading to frequent flu or colds*. There are also multiple psychological effects of stress, such as anxiety, panic attacks, pessimism, or, in the long term, depression. (Seaward, 2017)

Photo credit: Pixabay

7.7 DEMOTIVATION

Employees who are given too much work will not be motivated to complete it all, as even if they complete one task, it won't look like much progress has been made. They'll feel as if they're overwhelmed and will not be able to finish tasks on time.

This demotivation is especially true if the employee has more than one manager to answer to and complete tasks for. If all of them want their tasks to be done first, the employee may become too stressed to complete the work on time and will end up not getting much done.

Procrastination has a close relation with demotivation. Once you feel motivated to accomplish something, you'll never procrastinate at all because you have a clear and detailed goal for yourself. However, procrastination starts once you lose your passion and begin feeling depressed about the excessive work. Demotivation isn't a fault of the employees but a consequence of restricting the worker in a vicious cycle.

7.8 MISTAKES

An employee who has been given too much work won't be focusing 100% on every task they've been given. They may be too overwhelmed with work to do this. If an employee has been given a deadline that doesn't give them too much time to complete a task, they may make mistakes and not concentrate on every little detail as much as they should. The quality of the work may be sacrificed.

If an employee has too much work and no time for sleep, exercise, or cooking healthy meals, their job performance may get worse. They may become lazy, slack off, try to find short cuts within every task, and not be able to concentrate on their job properly. If an employee has to work every night until late, they may not be getting much sleep. This means they may not be able to get to early morning meetings or wake up in time for office hours. (Inegbedion, 2020)

Photo credit: Pixabay

7.9 COMPARISONS

An employee may compare their job with that of a friend or a family member. If they're earning about the same, and the same skill set is needed, they may consider applying for a job at the other firm if it involves less or no overwork.

7.10 PRESSURE

If an employee is being pressured too much into completing excessive amounts of work every single day, they definitely won't enjoy the work, even if they did so before when their workload was less. This means they'll do the work with less enthusiasm and, thus, may make more mistakes or take longer to complete it.

7.11 ALCOHOLISM

If an employee's job becomes so stressful that they have to turn to alcohol or drugs to relax after a long day, the chances of them being dissatisfied with their job are very high. Many people turn to alcohol or drugs as an outlet when they have too much work and resulting stress. This affects their relationships with family and friends and makes them less efficient at work. (Canfield & Andrews, 2016)

Workers tend to be easily exposed by the temptation of addictions. Alcohol and drugs become more appealing when the employees are exhausted from their excessive amount of work. It's hard to assign the fault of this entirely on the employees who became addicts and alcoholics.

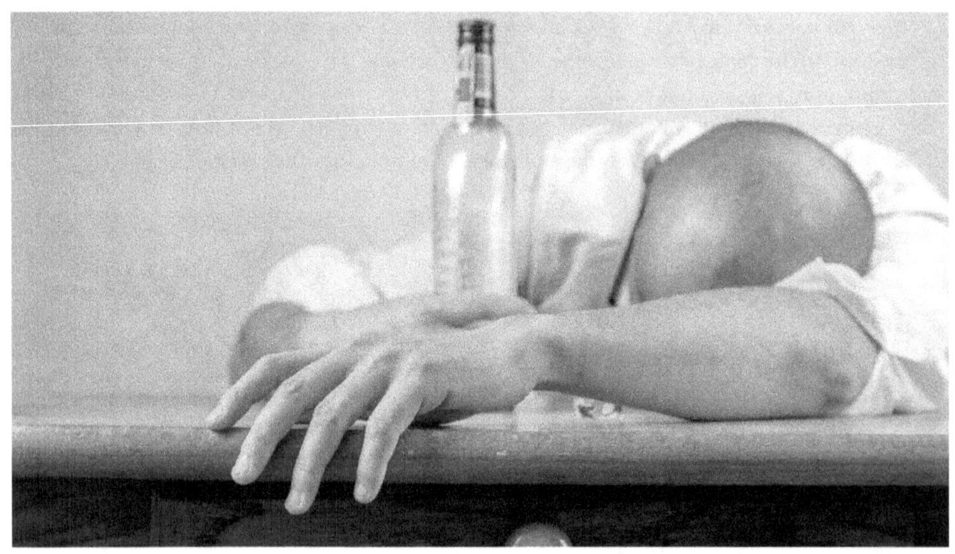

Photo credit: Pixabay

7.12 ISOLATION

If an employee has more work than they can handle at one time, they may be forced to sit at their desk all day and just work. Many employees often eat their lunch sitting at their desks because of the sheer amount of work they have. This will mean they don't have time to socialize with their colleagues, and may feel isolated, sitting in a room or cubicle all day long. (Sobia & Farooqi, 2014)

An employee can only be pushed so far until they become too overwhelmed with all the work that has been given to them and decide to quit their job.

An overworked employee is never a happy employee. Their job dissatisfaction will increase as time goes on if the excessive workload stays the same or increases. The employee may become less and less excited to come to work every morning, and their demotivation will keep increasing. This may be harmful to the company they work at too, as the quality of work will decrease, and the number of mistakes will increase.

Photo credit: Pixabay

Kindly note that this final image was inserted here because, even though the main theme of the picture is quarantine, it represents how people feel isolated and strongly desire the pre-pandemic normal life just as overworked employees desire a normal life.

CONCLUSION

Businesses should always value the quality of work over quantity because that's what really matters. If an employee has been given too many tasks to complete in a short amount of time, the quality of their work may decrease very sharply.

This could translate into a loss of revenue for a business, or their reputation being compromised in the market, as their products or services won't be of the same good quality as before.

Consistently having too much work to do almost always turns into a disaster story. Stress levels skyrocket, and many people experience physical as well as psychological symptoms that ultimately end up affecting their health. Strokes and heart attacks are very common results of stress caused by a heavy workload.

Employees won't have enough time to focus on their lives outside of work. They won't be able to go on jogs, spend time with their children, attend weddings or other functions, or just have some alone time to themselves. With so much work and more constantly piling up, they may become isolated and introverted with very little time to socialize with other people. However, employees can do many things to achieve a better work-life balance. They can get up from their desk every 20 minutes or so, stretch their legs and rest their eyes for 20 seconds, and then go back to work. This will help keep the employee healthy. Small breaks like these decrease stress levels astronomically.

Remember that it's okay to say no if your boss assigns you work when you already have way too much, or when your colleague asks you to help them out with a project. If it's harmful to your health and wellbeing, then it's definitely okay to say no.

It's important that we keep our health in mind when working. **Too much work can actually kill you.** So, be careful, and be thoughtful.

REFERENCES

Argenal, Sarah, *The Whole SELF Lifestyle for Working Parents: A Practical 4-Step Framework to Defeat Burnout and Escape Survival Mode for Good*, Argenal Institute LLC, https://amzn.to/3fEccl5, 2020.

Askin, Elizabeth, et. al., *The Health Care Handbook: A Clear & Concise Guide to the United States Health Care System*, Washington University Press in St. Louis, https://amzn.to/3dnR8hu, 2014.

Basil, Robert, *PRODUCTIVITY AT WORK: 36 tricks that will make you better at your job*, Amazon Services LLC, https://amzn.to/2YKLNeL, 2019.

Best10ResumeWriters, *How to Deal with Heavy Workload to Save Your Career*, https://www.businessinsider.com/why-investment-bankers-work-so-much-2012-10, 2019.

Brindle, Khara Croswaite, *Perfectioneur From Workaholic to Well-balanced: One Therapist's Guide to Get You There*, Amazon.com Services LLC, https://amzn.to/3ewZchf, 2020.

Brodie, Chris J., *Investment Banking Interview Questions and Answers Prep Guide (200 Q&As): Ace your technical questions and tell your unique story that will intrigue ... your background*, Independently Published, https://amzn.to/2Y8WE38, 2019.

Burchard, Brendon, *The High Performance Planner Diary – Project Calendar*, Hay House Inc. Publishers, https://amzn.to/2Nlp5Vd, 2018.

Burka, Jane B. and Lenora M. Yuen, *Procrastination: Why You Do It, What to Do About It Now*, Da Capo Lifelong Books, https://amzn.to/2CyfRD1, 2008.

Bush, Cathy and Tara Peters, *The Demotivated Employee: Helping Leaders Solve the Motivation Crisis That Is Plaguing Business*, Advantage Media Group, https://amzn.to/2zEO0zM, 2020.

Canfield, Jack and Dave Andrews, *The 30-day Sobriety Solution: How to Cut Back or Quit Drinking in the Privacy of Your Own Home*, Atria Books, https://amzn.to/3egHUnL, 2016.

Carbonell PhD, David A. and Sally M. Winston PsyD, *The Worry Trick: How Your Brain Tricks You into Expecting the Worst and What You Can Do About It*, New Harbinger Publications, https://amzn.to/317nCKo, 2016.

Carlton, Bob, *Fast Shingles Cure - How to Cure Shingles in 3 Days or Less: Learn a Proven Step-by-step Method to Cure Shingles in 3 Days or Less!*, Amazon Services LLC, https://amzn.to/2Z5v3PF, 2014.

Chiesa, Jorge O., *HOW TO EFFECTIVELY CURE CHRONIC WORK-RELATED STRESS: STOP STRESSING YOURSELF AT WORK, REMOVE ACUTE ANXIETY FROM YOUR LIFE QUICKLY, DEVELOP A POSITIVE ATTITUDE*, Amazon Services, LLC, https://amzn.to/2YtqWOl, 2019.

Clear, James, *Atomic Habits: An Easy & Proven Way to Build Good Habits & Break Bad Ones*, Avert Publishers, https://amzn.to/3hQEI59, 2018.

Cohen, Rebecca, *Fifteen Minutes Outside: 365 Ways to Get Out of the House and Connect with Your Kids*, Sourcebooks Publishers, https://amzn.to/2AZQ1Y5, 2011.

Cooper, Chayla, *5 Keys to Job Promotion: Through the Eyes of David and Goliath*, Sleeq Productions, https://amzn.to/3fAsj3o, 2020.

Crichton-Stuart, Cathleen, What Are Some Foods to Ease Your Anxiety?, *Medical News Today*, https://www.medicalnewstoday.com/articles/322652, 2018.

Csikszentmihalyi, Mihaly, *Beyond Boredom and Anxiety: Experiencing Flow in Work and Play*, Jossey-Bass, https://amzn.to/2YKF58r, 2000.

Dennis, Marcia, *Managing Priorities and Deadlines: 28 Secrets to Time Management Success*, SkillPath Publications, https://amzn.to/2YcaXUp, 2007.

Detjens, Beth, *Suddenly Home: A Quick Start Guide to Successfully Working from Home*, Amazon Services LLC, https://amzn.to/3drUhN2, 2020.

Devlin, Tara A., *Aokigahara: The Truth Behind Japan's Suicide Forest*, Independently Published, https://amzn.to/3g1vnG1, 2019.

DiFonzo, Sal, *Designing Effective Incentive Compensation Plans: Create a Plan That Drives Strategy, Engages Employees, and Achieves Success*, Createspace Publishers, https://amzn.to/3fATuLu, 2015.

Durand, Dave, *Perpetual Motivation: How to Light Your Fire and Keep It Burning in Your Career and in Life*, Franciscan Media, https://amzn.to/2O7dERj, 2011.

Eblin, Scott, *Overworked and Overwhelmed: The Mindfulness Alternative*, Wiley, https://amzn.to/2Z8ajrx, 2014.

Edwards, Jim, A Chinese Bank Regulator Died From Working Overtime — And Officials Applauded His Dedication, *Business Insider,* https://www.businessinsider.com/china-bank-regulator-li-jianhua-died-from-overwork-2014-6, 2014.

Employee Benefits, *The Top Three Causes of Workplace Stress and How to Solve Them*, https://employeebenefits.co.uk/top-three-causes-workplace-stress-solve/, 2017.

Felton, Danielle E., *Teach and Go Home: The Sophisticated Guide to Simplifying and Managing Your Workload and More*, Difference Press, https://amzn.to/2YnwEAX, 2020.

Feroli, Michael, *Finance and Economics Discussion Series: Capital Flows Among the G-7 Nations: A Demographic Perspective*, BiblioGov Publishers, https://amzn.to/37YW37c, 2013.

Gonzalez, John and Young Lee, *SOUTH KOREA: The Price of Efficiency and Success*, Independently Published, https://amzn.to/31kGgOK, 2019.

Hampshire, David, *Living and Working in Germany: A Survival Handbook (Living & Working)*, Survival Books Ltd., https://amzn.to/2A5pbNQ, 2017.

Haraway, Michele and Marsali Hansen, *Spouse Abuse: Assessing & Treating Battered Women, Batterers, & Their Children*, Professional Resource Publishers, https://amzn.to/3hTUewY, 2004.

Harrison, Milton, *Substance Abuse Opioids: Crisis, Addiction, and THE WAY OUT*, T. Tower LLC Publishers, https://amzn.to/3fJcpDC, 2020.

Harvard Business Review, *HBR Guide to Work-life Balance*, https://amzn.to/2YJB0Sa, 2019.

Hawkins, Logan, *Find Your Max: Improve Work Productivity with Time Management Magic (Quality Life Series)*, Amazon Services LLC, https://amzn.to/30RPa6h, 2020.

Iliaca, Peter, *Task Management through the Eisenhower Matrix: A Task Management Notebook*, Independently Published, https://amzn.to/3erbBD7, 2019.

Inegbedion, Henry, *Perception of Workload Balance and Employee Job Satisfaction in Work Organisations*, ScienceDirect, https://www.sciencedirect.com/science/article/pii/S2405844020300050, 2020.

Kelly, Erin L., *Overload: How Good Jobs Went Bad and What We Can Do about It*, Princeton University Press, https://amzn.to/2Cila9f, 2020.

Kennedy, James F., *The Influence of Outsourcing on Job Satisfaction and Turnover Intentions of Air Force Civil Engineer Company Grade Officers*, BiblioScholar, https://amzn.to/3edCBVL, 2012.

Khan, Mohammad Ayub and Laurie Smith Law, *The Role of National Cultures in Shaping the Corporate Management Cultures: A Three-country Theoretical Analysis*, IntechOpen, https://www.intechopen.com/books/organizational-culture/the-role-of-national-cultures-in-shaping-the-corporate-management-cultures-a-three-country-theoretic, 2018.

Kwon, Jake and Alexandra Field, South Koreans Are Working Themselves to Death. Can They Get Their Lives Back?, *CNN*, https://edition.cnn.com/2018/11/04/asia/korea-working-hours-intl/index.html, 2018.

Kyodo, Number of Newborns in Japan Fell to Record Low While Population Dropped Faster Than Ever in 2018, *Japan Times,* https://www.japantimes.co.jp/news/2019/06/07/national/number-newborns-japan-fell-low-918397-2018-government-survey/, 2019.

Le Parisien, *Suicide à France Telecom : « J'en Peux Plus », Avait Confié Jean-Paul à des Collègues*, https://www.leparisien.fr/archives/suicide-a-france-telecom-j-en-peux-plus-avait-confie-jean-paul-a-des-collegues-29-09-2009-655445.php, 2009.

Lim, Jessie, Dead for Dough: Death by Overwork Around the World, *Strait Times,* Https://Www.Straittimes.Com/World/Dead-For-Dough-Death-By-Overwork-Around-The-World, 2017.

Lopez, Alex, *Excessive Workload: Has Overwork Become the New Norm?,* RMI Solutions, https://rmi-solutions.com/excessive-workload/, 2017.

Maangchi and Martha Rose Shulman, *Maangchi's Big Book of Korean Cooking: From Everyday Meals to Celebration Cuisine,* Rux Martin/Houghton Mifflin Harcourt, https://amzn.to/2VcdOuI, 2019.

McCoy, Monica L. and Stefanie M. Keen, *Child Abuse and Neglect,* Psychology Press, https://amzn.to/2B2PeWd, 2013.

Meyer, Erin, *The Culture Map: Breaking through the Invisible Boundaries of Global Business,* Public Affairs Publishers, https://amzn.to/2Nsq8mg, 2014.

Miller, Sheldon, *The Healthy Smoothie Cookbook: Breakfast Smoothie, Body Cleansing Smoothies, Digestive Smoothies, Kid-friendly Smoothies, Low-fat Smoothies, Best Protein Smoothies, Easy to Make Weight loss Smoothies,* Independently Published, https://amzn.to/2NmUw1n, 2020.

Nagoski, Emily, *Burnout: The Secret to Unlocking the Stress Cycle,* Ballantine Books, https://amzn.to/2O28GFH, 2020.

Nanavati, Kaushal B., *CORE 4 of Wellness: Nutrition | Physical Exercise | Stress Management | Spiritual Wellness,* Amazon Services LLC, https://amzn.to/2Z2x3YT, 2016.

Necek, Barbara and Aline Hoorpah, *South Korea: Success at All Costs,* Patrick SPICA Productions, https://amzn.to/2NsVtVW, 2016.

Odimba, Kennedy King, *Living Beyond Limitations Everyday: Twelve Profound Principles on How to Live Beyond Your Limitations Every Day,* Fulton Books, https://amzn.to/315AnF5, 2020.

OECD, *Hours Worked,* OECD Employment Outlook, https://data.oecd.org/emp/hours-worked.htm, 2018.

Oosthuizen, R.M., et al. "Work-life Balance, Job Satisfaction and Turnover Intention amongst Information Technology Employees." *Southern African Business Review,* https://www.ajol.info/index.php/sabr/article/view/151750, 2016.

Oster, Shai, In China, 1,600 People Die Every Day from Working Too Hard: White-Collar Workers Are Dying from Overwork, *Bloomberg,* https://www.bloomberg.com/news/articles/2014-07-03/in-china-white-collar-workers-are-dying-from-overwork, 2014.

Pencavel, John H., *Diminishing Returns at Work: The Consequences of Long Working Hours,* Oxford University Press, https://amzn.to/2NnMvcs, 2018.

Peters, Kimberly, *How to Be a Good Manager: Easy Ways to Become a More Effective & Higher Producing Management Professional*, Createspace Publishers, https://amzn.to/3eauoCQ, 2014.

Roger, Derek and Nick Petrie, *Work without Stress: Building a Resilient Mindset for Lasting Success*, McGraw-Hill Education, https://amzn.to/2N9L1CI, 2016.

Safarova, Kristina, *Succeeding as a Management Consultant*, Independently Published, https://amzn.to/2BjDwpU, 2020.

Saiidi, Uptin, Japan Has Some of the Longest Working Hours in the World. It's Trying to Change, *CNBC*, https://www.cnbc.com/2018/06/01/japan-has-some-of-the-longest-working-hours-in-the-world-its-trying-to-change.html, 2018.

Sarva, Amol, Why Germans Work Fewer Hours but Produce More: A Study in Culture, *HuffPost*, https://www.huffpost.com/entry/why-germans-work-fewer-ho_b_6172262?guccounter=1&guce_referrer=aHR0cHM6Ly93d3cuZ29vZ2xlLmNvbS88&guce_referrer_sig=AQAAANKNQLXADpSx5UWMvgS5M1mjDzkxVYAKMRDQ5rfmWUMkxmL5G4PWVwB9hDi3tJM62c7XOWlo4fvy_o0qbhALRdvJXA6fPVKYzgfvF8Y_xJb1V2kzHVetCoeaPFCggl71dtLczj46KpR2Ak9rb-5wfysMRDb_5oDc2in-XCwAdU9, 2017.

Seaward, Brian Luke, *Managing Stress: Principles and Strategies for Health and Well-Being*, Jones & Bartlett Learning, https://amzn.to/2Zb5jme, 2017.

Segal, Jeanne, *Stress at Work*, Help Guide, https://www.helpguide.org/articles/stress/stress-in-the-workplace.htm, 2020.

Sehnert, Keith W., *Stress/Unstress: How You Can Control Stress at Home and on the Job*, Augsburg Fortress Pub, https://amzn.to/2Ar1H64, 1981.

Smith, Nicola, *South Koreans Forced to Relax under New Overtime Rules Limiting Working Week to 52 hours*, Telegraph UK, https://www.telegraph.co.uk/news/2018/07/02/south-koreans-forced-relax-new-overtime-rules-limiting-working/, 2018.

Sobia, Ali and Yasir Farooqi, *Effect of Work Overload on Job Satisfaction, Effect of Job Satisfaction on Employee Performance and Employee Engagement*, Research Gate, https://www.researchgate.net/publication/324647967_Effect_of_Work_Overload_on_Job_Satisfaction_Effect_of_Job_Satisfaction_on_Employee_Performance_and_Employee_Engagement_A_Case_of_Public_Sector_University_of_Gujranwala_Division, 2014.

Strait Times, *South Korea Officially Drops Its Maximum Workweek to 52 Hours to Promote Work-Life Balance*, https://www.straitstimes.com/asia/east-asia/south-korea-officially-drops-its-maximum-workweek-to-52-hours, 2018.

Telegraph UK, *French Win Right Disconnect Out of Hours Work Emails*, https://www.telegraph.co.uk/news/2016/12/31/french-win-right-disconnect-out-of-hours-work-emails/, 2016.

Telegraph UK, *Out of Hours Working Banned by German Labour Ministry*, https://www.telegraph.co.uk/news/worldnews/europe/germany/10276815/Out-of-hours-working-banned-by-German-labour-ministry.html, 2020.

Thomas, Kenneth W., *Intrinsic Motivation at Work: Building Energy and Commitment*, Berrett-Koehler Publishers, https://amzn.to/2NaksNz, 2009

Traub, Andy, *The Early to Rise Experience: Learn to Rise Early in 30 Days*, Take Permission Media Network Publishers, https://amzn.to/3erEH5w, 2013.

Weber, A., and A. Jaekel-Reinhard. "Burnout Syndrome: A Disease of Modern Societies?" OUP Academic, Oxford University Press, https://academic.oup.com/occmed/article/50/7/512/1444456, 1 Sept. 2000.

Weisinger, Hendrie and J. P. Pawliw-Fry, *Performing Under Pressure: The Science of Doing Your Best When It Matters Most*, Currency Publishers, https://amzn.to/2zKCFOQ, 2015.

Wilkinson, Richard and Kate Pickett, *The Inner Level: How More Equal Societies Reduce Stress, Restore Sanity and Improve Everyone's Well-being*, Penguin Books, https://amzn.to/3dmwdv3, 2020.

Wilson, Pearl, *Work-life Balance*, Business Culture, https://businessculture.org/western-europe/business-culture-in-france/work-life-balance-in-france/, 2019.

Yutaka, Matsushige and Masayuki Qusumi, *Japanese Drama: Kodoku No Gurume, Kodoku No Gourmet w/ English Subtitle*, https://amzn.to/2YypFWd, 2012.

Zahariades, Damon, *To-Do List Formula: A Stress-Free Guide to Creating To-Do Lists That Work!*, Damon Zahariades Publishers, https://amzn.to/3fPlsTA, 2016.

Zahariades, Damon, *The Art of Saying NO: How to Stand Your Ground, Reclaim Your Time and Energy, and Refuse to Be Taken for Granted (Without Feeling Guilty!)*, Independently Published, https://amzn.to/2YqdM4l, 2017.